CALL to CELEBRATE EUCHARIST

This book belongs to

Ryan Glascock

Harcourt Religion Publishers

Author
Maureen A. Kelly, M.A.

Nihil Obstat
Msgr. Louis R. Piermarini
Imprimatur
✢Most Rev. Robert J. McManus, S.T.D.
Bishop of Worcester
August 9, 2005

The Ad Hoc Committee to Oversee the Use of the Catechism, United States Conference of Catholic Bishops, has found this catechetical text, copyright ©2007, to be in conformity, as a supplemental catechetical material, with the *Catechism of the Catholic Church.*

For permission to reprint copyrighted material, grateful acknowledgment is made to the following sources:

Michael Balhoff: Lyrics from "We Praise You" by Mike Balhoff, Darryl Ducote, and Gary Daigle. Lyrics © 1978 by Damean Music.

John Burland: Lyrics from "Yes Lord I Believe!" by John Burland. Lyrics © 2000 by John Burland. Lyrics from "Come to the Table" by John Burland. Lyrics © 2005 by John Burland.

Division of Christian Education of the National Council of the Churches of Christ in the U.S.A.: Scripture quotations from the *New Revised Standard Version Bible: Catholic Edition.* Text copyright © 1993 and 1989 by the Division of Christian Education of the National Council of the Churches of Christ in the U.S.A.

GIA Publications, Inc., 7404 S. Madison Ave., Chicago, IL 60638, www.giamusic.com, 800-442-1358: "I Will Praise You, Lord"/"Te alabaré Señor" by Tony Alonso. Lyrics © 2003 by GIA Publications, Inc.

International Commission on English in the Liturgy: From the English translation of "Blessing After Meals" in *Book of Blessings.* Translation © 1988 by International Committee on English in the Liturgy, Inc. From the English translation of the *Rite of Christian Initiation of Adults.* Translation © 1985 by International Committee on English in the Liturgy, Inc. From the English translation of *The Roman Missal.* Translation © 1973 by International Committee on English in the Liturgy, Inc. From the English translation of "Come, Holy Spirit" in *A Book of Prayers.* Translation © 1982 by International Committee on English in the Liturgy, Inc. From the English translation of Psalm Refrains in *Lectionary for Mass.* Translation © 1969, 1981, 1997 by International Committee on English in the Liturgy, Inc.

International Consultation on English Texts: English translation of Hail Mary, Gloria in Excelsis, and the Apostles' Creed by the International Consultation on English Texts (ICET).

OCP Publications, 5536 NE Hassalo, Portland, OR 97213: Lyrics from "Lead Us to the Water" by Tom Kendzia, Gary Daigle, and John Foley. Lyrics © 1998 by Tom Kendzia, Gary Daigle, and John Foley. Lyrics from "Open My Eyes" by Jesse Manibusan. Lyrics © 1988 by Jesse Manibusan.

Illustration Credits
Dan Brown/Artworks 36–37; Shane Marsh/Linden Artists, Ltd. 6–7, 56–57; Roger Payne/Linden Artists, Ltd. 26–27; Francis Phillips/Linden Artists, Ltd. 76–77; Tracy Somers 10, 11, 21, 60, 80, 81; Clive Spong/Linden Artists, Ltd.16–17, 46–47, 66–67.

Photo Credits
Laurent Emmanuel/Corbis Sygma 18.

Printed in the United States of America

ISBN: 0-15-901639-8

4 5 6 7 8 9 10   059   10 09 08 07

Contents

Dear Child,

This is a very special time for you. You are preparing to take another step in your journey of friendship with Jesus and the Church. Your journey began when you were baptized. This journey of faith never ends. You will keep growing in your friendship with Jesus and the Church for your whole life.

In some parishes, children celebrate the Sacrament of Confirmation before receiving Holy Communion for the first time. In other parishes, children receive Holy Communion and then, when they are older, they celebrate the Sacrament of Confirmation.

What sacraments will you be celebrating this year?

_____

_____

During this time, you will

- learn about the Sacraments of Initiation
- pray with your friends and family
- listen to the stories of Jesus and the Apostles
- learn about the parts of the Mass
- prepare to celebrate the sacraments

What is your favorite part of the Mass?

_____

_____

What are you looking forward to learning this year?

_____

_____

My Faith Journey

I was baptized on _____ at _____.

My godparents are _____.

I was baptized by _____.

I was confirmed on _____ at _____.

My sponsor was _____.

I was confirmed by _____.

I celebrated Reconciliation for the first time on _____

at _____.

I celebrated my First Communion on _____

at _____ .

_____ presided at the Eucharist.

Some of the people who helped me prepare for First Communion were

_____

_____

What I remember most about preparing for my First Communion

_____

_____

What I remember most about my First Communion Day

_____

_____

1 We Belong

We Gather

Procession

As you sing, walk forward slowly.
Follow the person carrying the Bible.

 Sing together.

I believe in God the Father
I believe in God the Son
I believe in the Spirit
And the strength that makes
us one.

© 2000 John Burland

Leader: Let us pray.

Make the Sign of the Cross
together.

Ritual Focus: Renewal of Baptismal Promises

Leader: On the day of your
Baptism, your family
and the Church claimed
you for Christ.

You received the gifts
of faith and new life.
Today let us remember
the promises of
Baptism together.

Come forward, and gather
around the water and candle.

Leader: Do you say "no" to sin, so
that you can live always
as God's children?

All: I do.

Leader: Do you believe in God,
the Father almighty?

All: I do.

Leader: Do you believe in Jesus
Christ, his only Son,
our Lord?

All: I do.

Leader: Do you believe in the Holy Spirit, the holy catholic Church, the communion of saints?

All: I do.

Leader: This is our faith. This is the faith of the Church. We are proud to profess it in Christ Jesus.

All: Amen.

BASED ON RITE OF BAPTISM FOR CHILDREN 144–146

Leader: Let us come to the water and thank God for the gift of our Baptism.

One at a time, make the Sign of the Cross with the water.

[Name], you are the light of Christ.

Child: Amen.

We Listen

Leader: God, our Father, open our hearts to the Holy Spirit as we remember our Baptism. We ask this through Jesus Christ our Lord.

All: Amen.

Leader: A reading from the holy Gospel according to John.

All: Glory to you, Lord.

Leader: Read John 15:1–17.

The Gospel of the Lord.

All: Praise to you, Lord Jesus Christ.

Sit silently.

We Go Forth

Leader: Loving God, we thank you for the gift of Baptism. Send us forth to bring your love to others. We ask this through Jesus Christ our Lord.

All: Amen.

 Sing the opening song together.

New Life

SIGNS OF FAITH

Water

Water gives life. It cleans and makes things like new. Water also reminds us of new life. The water used at Baptism is blessed. The blessed water is a sign that God the Father gives us his life and cleanses us from all sin. Through the waters of Baptism, we have new life with Jesus. Every time we go into a church, we bless ourselves with holy water. We remember our Baptism.

Reflect

Renewal of Promises Think and write about the celebration.

When I said, "I do"

_____

_____

_____

When I put my hand in water

_____

_____

_____

When I heard the words "the light of Christ"

_____

_____

_____

The Body of Christ

Baptism makes us children of God and members of the Church, the **Body of Christ**. At Baptism, we are given new life with Jesus Christ. **Original sin** and all personal sins are forgiven. We receive the light of Christ and become his followers. People who follow Jesus are called disciples. Another name for a follower of Christ is *Christian*.

Through our Baptism, we belong to the Church and become special friends of God. We need Baptism to have life with God forever.

In Baptism, God the Holy Spirit comes to live in us. The Holy Spirit

- helps us believe and have faith

- shows us how to pray

- guides us to be the light of Christ for others and makes us holy

- helps us follow God's law

SIGNS OF FAITH

The Paschal Candle
Sometimes this candle is called the Easter Candle. Every year at the Easter Vigil, a new candle is lit from the Easter fire. The candle is lit at all the Masses during the Easter season and at all Baptisms and funerals. During Baptism, the priest or deacon uses the **Paschal Candle** to light the candles of those being baptized.

We Belong to God

Faith Focus

What does Jesus tell us about belonging to God?

Jesus knew he would be returning to God, his Father. Jesus' disciples were sad. They wanted to stay close to him. Jesus wanted to tell his friends that he would always be with them. He wanted them to know that they belonged to him in a special way. So, he told them this story.

Scripture

JOHN 15:1–17

The Vine and the Branches

"I am the true vine, and my Father is the vine grower. He takes away every branch in me that does not bear fruit. Every branch that does bear fruit, he cuts back so it will grow more fruit. A branch cannot bear fruit on its own. It must remain on the vine. You are the branches of the vine. As long as you stay close to me, you will keep bearing fruit."

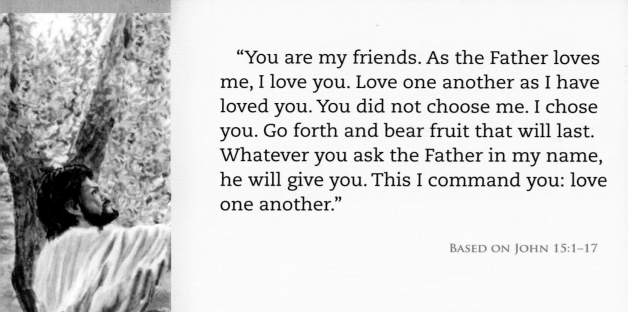

"You are my friends. As the Father loves me, I love you. Love one another as I have loved you. You did not choose me. I chose you. Go forth and bear fruit that will last. Whatever you ask the Father in my name, he will give you. This I command you: love one another."

BASED ON JOHN 15:1–17

❓ **What was Jesus telling his friends in this story?**

❓ **How is Jesus your friend? How are you his friend?**

Faith at Home

Read the scripture story with your child. Talk about ways that you stay close to Jesus. Decide on one activity you can do to stay close to Jesus while your child is preparing to receive Holy Communion.

Share

Draw a picture On a sheet of paper, draw a picture of one way you can show others that you belong to God.

The Sacraments of Initiation

SIGNS OF FAITH

The Holy Trinity

The mystery of one God in three Persons: Father, Son, and Holy Spirit is called the Trinity (*CCC.* Glossary). The three Persons act together in all they do, but each Person also has a special role. We sometimes call God the Father the Creator because he made everything. Jesus Christ is the Son of God and our Savior. God the Holy Spirit makes us holy. Each Person of the Trinity is called God.

Faith Focus

Which sacraments are signs of belonging?

A **sacrament** is an outward sign that comes from Jesus. Sacraments give us grace, a share in God's life. Baptism, Confirmation, and Eucharist are called **Sacraments of Initiation**. We are joined closely to Christ through these sacraments. They make us members of the Catholic Church. They are signs that we belong to God and to the Church.

Baptism

In Baptism the priest or deacon pours water over our head or lowers us into the water three times. He says, "I baptize you in the name of the Father, and of the Son, and of the Holy Spirit." Then he rubs blessed oil on our head. This is called anointing. We need to be baptized only one time.

As a sign of our new life in Christ, we receive a white garment. Then the priest or deacon gives our parent or godparent a lighted candle. He prays that we will walk as children of the light and follow Jesus' example.

Confirmation

The Sacrament of **Confirmation** strengthens God's life in us. Confirmation completes our Baptism and helps us grow as followers of Jesus. During Confirmation, the bishop or priest puts his hand out and prays:

"Send your Holy Spirit upon them
    to be their Helper and Guide."

Then the bishop or priest lays his hand on our heads and anoints us with the holy oil of **chrism**. Oil is a sign of strength. He says:

"Be sealed with the Gift of the Holy Spirit."

These words tell us that we receive the Holy Spirit in a special way at Confirmation. Both Baptism and Confirmation mark us with a special character that shows we belong to Jesus.

Eucharist

The Sacrament of the **Eucharist** joins us to Jesus in a special way. The Eucharist is a sacred meal of thanksgiving. Jesus shares his own Body and Blood with us in Holy Communion.

You participate in the Eucharist by coming to Mass with your family.

❓ **How are the Sacraments of Initiation signs of belonging?**

9

Children of Light

Respond

Describe a disciple In the banner below, color in the words "Child of the Light." Then write words that describe a follower of Jesus.

_____

_____

_____

Closing Blessing

Gather and begin with the Sign of the Cross.

Leader: God, our Father, we thank you for choosing us to be your children.

All: Amen.

Leader: Jesus, the Son of God, we thank you for showing us how to live.

All: Amen.

Leader: Holy Spirit, giver of God's gifts, we praise and thank you for guiding us.

 Sing together.

I believe in God the Father
I believe in God the Son
I believe in the Spirit
And the strength that makes us one.

© 2000 John Burland

Faith at Home

Faith Focus

- A sacrament is an outward sign that comes from Jesus and gives us grace.

- Baptism, Confirmation, and Eucharist are called Sacraments of Initiation.

- The Sacraments of Initiation make us members of the Church.

Ritual Focus

Renewal of Baptismal Promises

The celebration focused on the Renewal of Baptismal Promises. The children renewed their baptismal promises. During the week, use the text on pages 2–3, and renew your own baptismal promises with your child and the rest of the family.

Act

Share Together   Read John 15:1–17. Talk about what actions show we are friends of Jesus. Using a shoe box, create a "Friends of Jesus" box. Invite family members to look for examples of how others are acting as friends of Jesus, write the examples on pieces of paper, and place them in the box. At the end of the week, read the slips of paper and share what you have learned.

Do Together   When discussing your child's Baptism, talk about all of the things you did to prepare for his or her birth. Point out that some babies are born into families who do not have the means to prepare for them. Discuss what you and your child could do to help. (Suggestions: Buy baby food or diapers for a homeless shelter, or pray for these children at a specific time every day.)

Family Prayer

God, our Father, thank you for making us your children. We believe in you and we belong to you. We ask you to keep us close to you. Show us how to love each other as you have loved us. Amen.

2 We Gather

We Gather

Ritual Focus: Procession and Gloria

As you sing, walk forward slowly.
Follow the person carrying the Bible.

🎼 Sing together.

Glory to God in the highest,
and peace to his people on earth.
Glory to God in the highest,
and peace to his people on earth.

©1987 GIA Publications, Inc.

Leader: Let us pray.

Make the Sign of the Cross
together.

God, our Loving Father,
we praise you for your
goodness and thank you

for the gift of your Son,
Jesus. Send us your Holy
Spirit to help us live as
your children. We ask
this through Jesus Christ
our Lord.

All: Amen.

Leader: Every Sunday we come
together as God's people
to praise him and to give
him thanks for everything
he has done. Today we do
the same.

Come forward, and gather around
the holy water and candle.

Lord Jesus, you came to
gather all people into your
Father's kingdom.

All: We give you glory and
thanks.

Leader: Lord Jesus, you came to
bring us new life.

All: We give you glory and thanks.

Leader: Lord Jesus, you came to save us.

All: We give you glory and thanks.

Leader: Let us give praise and thanks to God.

We Listen

Leader: God, our Father, you alone are holy. We ask you to help us be grateful children who always remember your glory. We ask this through Jesus Christ our Lord.

All: Amen.

Leader: A reading from the Acts of the Apostles.

Read Acts 2:42–47.

The word of the Lord.

All: Thanks be to God.

Sit silently.

We Go Forth

Leader: God, the Holy Spirit, we praise you and thank you for your gifts. May we act in ways that show your gifts to others. We ask this through Jesus Christ our Lord.

All: Amen.

 Sing the opening song together.

Gathered Together

SIGNS OF FAITH

Assembly

Many different people come together at Mass. Each person comes to praise and give thanks to God and to ask for his blessings. When we gather together to give God thanks and praise, we are an **assembly** of people who believe in Jesus. When the assembly gathers, God is there.

Reflect

Procession and Gloria   Draw a picture of what you want to thank and praise God for.

We Come Together

Every time we gather as a group, we come together to pray. When we begin to form the **procession** for our celebration, we are gathering for prayer. **Prayer** is talking and listening to God. The procession gathers us as a community ready for prayer.

During the Mass, we pray in many different ways. When we stand, we pray a prayer of reverence. Prayers can be said. We can say the Lord Have Mercy. We can ask for God's help. Prayers can be sung. We can sing the Glory to God in Mass. We pray in silence during the Mass, too. One time we pray in silence is after the Gospel reading.

SIGNS OF FAITH

Procession

A procession is a group of people moving forward as part of a celebration. Processions at Mass remind us that we are walking with God and that God is walking with us. At Mass the priest and other ministers come into the church in a procession. People bring the gifts to the altar in a procession. We walk in a procession to receive Jesus in Holy Communion.

15

We Gather As God's People

Faith Focus

What is a community of faith?

The early followers of Jesus gathered often to pray and to remember him. They were like a family. Their faith in Jesus made them a community of faith.

ACTS 2:42–47

The Early Christians

The members of the early Christian community gathered together over and over again. They got to know one another. They studied the teachings of the Apostles. Every day they went to the Temple to pray just as they had before they knew Jesus. On Sunday they gathered at one of their homes. In their homes they broke bread and prayed together. They shared the Lord's Body and Blood.

The early followers of Jesus shared their belongings with one another. They sold their property and possessions and made sure everyone had what they needed. Every time they ate together, they gave praise and thanks to God. They were very joyful. When other people saw how happy the followers of Jesus were, they wanted to join their community. They wanted to believe in Jesus and follow him.

BASED ON ACTS 2:42–47

? **How were the early Christians a community of faith?**

? **How is your Church a community of faith?**

Faith at Home

Read the scripture story with your child. Explain that many early Christians were Jewish and went to the Temple. Point out that the early Christians did not have church buildings. Talk about the ways your family and parish take care of the needs of other Christians.

Share

Write a play   With a partner, prepare a play showing one thing you do because you belong to a community of faith. Act out the play for the class.

The People Gather

SIGNS OF FAITH

Prayer and Singing

Singing is a way to pray. When we sing during Mass, we lift our minds, hearts, and voices to praise God in a special way. The whole assembly sings songs and hymns. Sometimes the choir sings and the assembly listens. The priest sometimes sings parts of the Mass.

Faith Focus

What happens when we gather as a community of faith?

Like the first Christians, we celebrate the Eucharist with a community, too. Our faith community is our Church family. During Mass we come together as the Body of Christ. Every Saturday evening or Sunday, we gather with our parish community for the celebration of Mass.

Sunday is an important day for Christians. Jesus rose from the dead on Easter Sunday. It is so important that the Church requires us to participate in Sunday Mass every week. We come together as an assembly on Sunday to give God thanks and praise, to listen to God's word, and to ask for his blessing. We also remember Jesus' death, Resurrection, and Ascension and share the Lord's Body and Blood. Then we are sent forth to live as Jesus' followers.

When we gather for Mass, we greet one another. We share our joy as we sing and pray.

Introductory Rites

The prayers and actions that begin the Mass are called the Introductory Rites. The Introductory Rites help us turn our hearts and minds to the great celebration of the Eucharist. The priest leads the assembly in the celebration of the Mass. Mass begins when he walks in procession to the altar. All of us in the assembly stand and sing.

The priest greets us. He often says "The Lord be with you," or similar words. We answer "And also with you." We know that God the Father, his Son, Jesus, and the Holy Spirit are with us. Together we thank God for his goodness.

❓ How do we show we are united as we gather for the Mass?

Give Praise and Thanks

Respond

Make a list   In the space below, make a list of reasons you want to give God praise and thanks.

1. _____

2. _____

3. _____

Closing Blessing

Gather and begin with the Sign of the Cross.

Leader: God, our Father, we praise and thank you for gathering us as your children. Send us your Holy Spirit to increase our faith and make our community strong.

We ask this in the name of Jesus Christ our Lord.

All: Amen.

Leader: Go in peace to love and serve the Lord.

All: Thanks be to God.

Sing together.

Glory to God in the highest,
and peace to his people on earth.
Glory to God in the highest,
and peace to his people on earth.

Faith at Home

Faith Focus

- The Church is the People of God and the Body of Christ.

- The Eucharist, or Mass, is the Church's most important action of praise and thanks.

- The Introductory Rites gather us as a community of faith.

Ritual Focus
Procession and Gloria

The celebration focused on the Procession and Gloria. The children sang the Gloria and prayed a litany of glory and praise to God. During the week, pray and talk about the meaning of the verses of the Gloria found on page 12.

Act

Share Together   Read Acts 2:42–47. Talk about what it must have been like for the early Christians to live as a community of faith. Emphasize the sharing of their possessions and their prayer life. Decide one way your family can continue to live as a community of faith, such as going to Mass or sharing your time and talents with others.

Pray Together   Together, make a list of all the things you want to thank God for. Read the list as a litany. One person prays, "For sun and rain," and everyone responds, "We thank you, God." During the weeks ahead, select appropriate times to pray a thanksgiving prayer with your child or family.

Litany

Family Prayer

Loving God, we are your people. Thank you for the gift of faith. Help us grow closer as a family. Strengthen our faith in you. Amen.

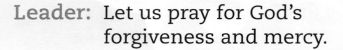
We Are Forgiven

We Gather

Ritual Focus: Penitential Rite

 Sing together.

Create in me a clean heart,
O God.
A clean heart, O God, create
in me.

©Tom Kendzia

Leader: Let us pray.

**Make the Sign of the
Cross together.**

Confiteor

Leader: God wants us to be united
with him. Let us think
about the times we have
not been united to God
or others.

Sit silently.

Leader: Let us pray for God's
forgiveness and mercy.

**Come forward, and gather around
the holy water and candle.**

All: I confess to almighty God,
and to you, my brothers
and sisters, that I have
sinned through my own
fault in my thoughts and
in my words, in what I
have done, and in what I
have failed to do; and I ask
blessed Mary, ever virgin,
all the angels and saints,
and you, my brothers and
sisters, to pray for me to
the Lord our God.

Leader: May God forgive us our sins
and make us united with
him and one another.

We Listen

Leader: God, our loving Father, you call us to forgiveness and peace. You want us to be united in you. Help us forgive others as you forgive us. We ask this through Jesus Christ our Lord.

All: Amen.

Leader: A reading from the holy Gospel according to Matthew.

All: Glory to you, Lord.

Leader: Read Matthew 9:9–13.

The Gospel of the Lord.

All: Praise to you, Lord Jesus Christ.

Sit silently.

We Go Forth

Leader: Let us offer each other the Sign of Peace.

Give the Sign of Peace to one another.
Say: "The Peace of the Lord be with you."
Answer: "And also with you."

Go forth united in God's love.

All: Amen.

 Sing the opening song together.

23

God's Forgiveness

SIGNS OF FAITH

Lord Have Mercy

Sometimes in the Mass, during the Penitential Rite, we say the prayer Lord Have Mercy. These are the words that people say to Jesus when they ask him to heal them. When we pray these words at Mass, we ask Jesus to heal and forgive our sins and the sins of the world. We want everyone to be forgiven and united to God and one another forever.

Reflect

Confiteor Draw the story of a time when you said, "I am sorry," and the other person said, "I forgive you."

"I am sorry."

"I forgive you."

We Are One

Just as our parents want our family to be united, or joined together, God wants us to be united to him. When we gather for Mass, we remember that God wants us to love and care for each other.

But sometimes we do not show love to others. In the beginning of the Mass, we say a prayer to show we are sorry. We tell God and the Church family, "I am sorry." We ask forgiveness. We are united with God and our church family.

SIGNS OF FAITH

Silence

There are special times of quiet at Mass. These times of silence unite us to God. During the silent times, we talk to God in our hearts. We keep our minds and hearts open to what God may be sharing with us.

Jesus Calls Sinners

Faith Focus

Why did Jesus eat with sinners?

Jesus made friends with people who had turned away from God. He ate and drank with them. He wanted them to know that God, his Father, welcomed them and wanted to be one with them.

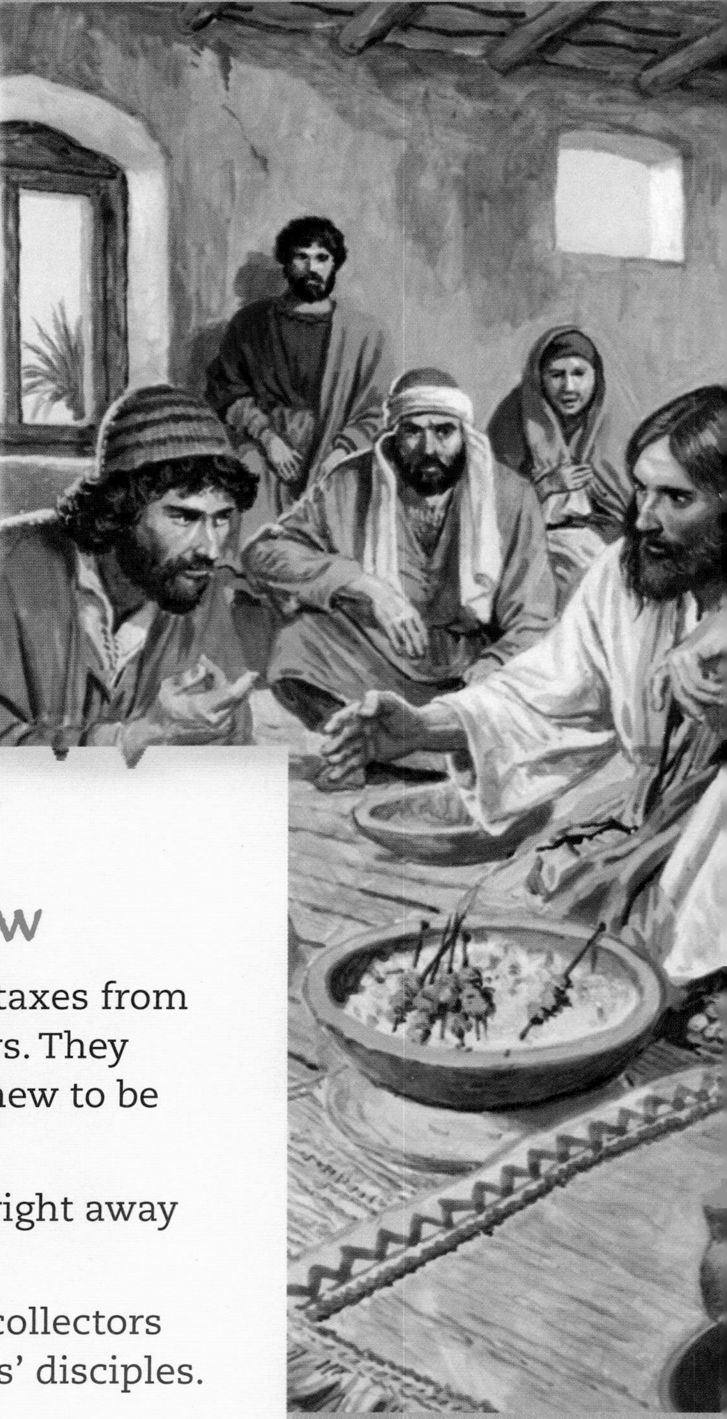

MATTHEW 9:9–13

Scripture

The Call of Matthew

One day Jesus saw Matthew, a tax collector, collecting taxes from the people. Many Jewish people did not like tax collectors. They would not be friends with them. But Jesus wanted Matthew to be his friend.

Jesus said, "Matthew, follow me." Matthew left his job right away and followed Jesus.

Later, Jesus had dinner at Matthew's house. Many tax collectors and sinners came and ate with Matthew, Jesus, and Jesus' disciples.

The Pharisees were Jewish leaders and teachers. They saw Jesus eating with sinners and tax collectors. They asked Jesus' disciples, "Why does your teacher eat with these people?"

When Jesus heard their question, he said, "I eat with them because I came to call sinners to be one with my Father."

BASED ON MATHEW 9:9–13

❓ **How do you think Matthew felt when Jesus asked him to become a follower?**

❓ **What do Jesus' words tell you?**

Faith at Home

Read the scripture story with your child. Point out situations in your child's family or school life in which someone may feel left out. Talk about ways you and your child can reach out to that person.

Share

Write a rhyme Write a sentence that rhymes with this:

Jesus always welcomes me.

_____

_____

Penitential Rite

SIGNS OF FAITH

Sprinkling with Holy Water
During some Sunday Masses, the priest walks through the church and sprinkles the assembly with holy water. The sprinkling reminds us of our Baptism. When the priest does the sprinkling with water, it takes the place of the Penitential Rite.

Faith Focus

What happens during the Penitential Rite?

Like the sinners in Jesus' time, sometimes we need Jesus to call us back to loving his Father.

- We may do things that hurt others.
- We may not do things that help people.
- We may not follow God's law by doing what we know is wrong.

When we do these things, we are not at one with God or others. But when we come to Mass to share a meal with Jesus, Jesus welcomes us. It is a time to become one again with God and others. The Eucharist is a sacrament of forgiveness and unity. However, anyone who has not confessed mortal sins must receive the Sacrament of Penance before participating in the Eucharist.

We Are Sorry

After the opening song and greeting, we pray together for God's forgiveness during the Penitential Rite. We ask God to make us one again. The priest invites us to remember our sins and be sorry for them.

We pray the Confiteor, a prayer of sorrow that begins with the words, "I confess." Sometimes we also pray the Lord Have Mercy. When we do this, the priest prays three prayers to Jesus, and we answer him. We pray, "Lord, have mercy, Christ, have mercy, Lord, have mercy." At the end of the Penitential Rite, the priest says this prayer:

"May almighty God have mercy on us, forgive us our sins, and bring us to everlasting life."

After the Penitential Rite, the Holy Spirit continues to unite us as an assembly. The Introductory Rites end. We are now ready to listen to God's word.

❓ **Why do you think the Penitential Rite is important?**

Faith at Home

Reinforce with your child the meaning of the Penitential Rite. Use examples from your family of times when someone asked forgiveness of others. Point out that relationships grow and are strengthened when people ask for and receive forgiveness. Use pages 22–23 to help your child learn the responses and prayers for the Penitential Rite.

We Forgive

Respond

Make a bulletin board about ways we forgive at home, school, and at church.

Closing Blessing

Gather and begin with the Sign of the Cross.

Leader: God, our Father, we praise and thank you for being a God who forgives.

All: Amen.

Leader: Jesus, our Savior, we praise and thank you for welcoming sinners and showing us how to live and love.

All: Amen.

Leader: Holy Spirit, giver of God's gifts, we praise and thank you for giving us courage to say "I am sorry" and to forgive others.

All: Amen.

♪ Sing together.

Create in me a clean heart, O God.

A clean heart, O God, create in me.

©Tom Kendzia

Faith at Home

Faith Focus

- The Eucharist is a sacrament of unity and forgiveness.
- Sin keeps us from being one People of God.
- At Mass we ask God's forgiveness during the Penitential Rite.

Ritual Focus

Penitential Rite The celebration focused on the Penitential Rite. The children prayed the Confiteor. During the week pray the Confiteor with your child.

Act

Share Together Saying "I am sorry" and "I forgive you" are important moments in the life of a family. Asking for and giving forgiveness can strengthen relationships. Sometimes, we seek forgiveness in indirect ways, by doing something special for the person we hurt. Have each family member draw a picture of one way they have seen a family member forgive another. Invite family members to share the story behind the picture.

Pray Together Admitting we have hurt one another and saying "I am sorry" are not always easy things to do. Choose a time to gather for prayer. Open with a prayer to the Holy Spirit. Invite family members to ask for, give, and receive forgiveness for the times they may have hurt one another during the week.

Family Prayer

God of Mercy, thank you for always forgiving us. By the power of the Holy Spirit, help us to change and become more like your Son, Jesus. Make us one in love with you and all the people in our lives. Amen.

4 We Listen

We Gather

Procession

As you sing, walk forward slowly.
Follow the person carrying the Bible.

 Sing together.

Open my ears, Lord.

Help me to hear your voice.

Open my ears, Lord.

Help me to hear.

© 1998, Jesse Manibusan.
Published by OCP Publications

Leader: Let us pray.

Make the Sign of the
Cross together.

We Listen

Leader: Father, send the Holy
Spirit to open our ears
and hearts that we may
hear and live your
word. We ask this in
Jesus' name.

All: Amen.

Leader: A reading from the
holy Gospel according
to Matthew.

All: Glory to you, Lord.

Ritual Focus: Signing

Leader: Loving Father, we want to
live by your word.

May your word be in
our minds.

Trace the Sign of the Cross on
your forehead.

Leader: May your word be on our lips.

Trace the Sign of the Cross on your lips.

May your word be in our hearts.

Trace the Sign of the Cross on your heart.

We ask this through Jesus Christ our Lord.

All: Amen.

Leader: Read Matthew 13:1–23.

The Gospel of the Lord.

All: Praise to you, Lord Jesus Christ.

Sit silently.

We Go Forth

Leader: Loving God, we thank you for your word. Help us remember and share it. We ask this through Jesus Christ our Lord.

All: Amen.

 Sing the opening song together.

God's Word

SIGNS OF FAITH

The Sign of the Cross

Each of us is signed with the Sign of the Cross at our Baptism. The Sign of the Cross marks us as followers of Jesus. Every time we sign ourselves with the Sign of the Cross, we remember our Baptism. In Baptism we are called to be disciples who follow God's word.

Reflect

Signing   Think and write about the celebration.

When God's word is in my mind

_____

_____

_____

When God's word is on my lips

_____

_____

_____

When God's word is in my heart

_____

_____

_____

The Bible

We know that the **Bible** is God's own word. Another name used for the Bible is Scriptures. The word *Scriptures* means "writings." God inspired humans to write stories of his love and friendship. At Mass we listen to and remember those stories. The good news of the Bible is the same good news that Jesus taught.

God the Father, Son, and Holy Spirit are with us when we pray for God's word to be in our minds, on our lips, and in our hearts. They help us hear the good news and share it with others.

SIGNS OF FAITH

The Bible

The Bible has two parts. The parts of the Bible are the Old Testament and the New Testament. The Old Testament tells stories of the friendship between God and his people before the birth of Jesus. The New Testament tells the stories of Jesus and the people in the early Church.

Hear God's Word

Faith Focus

Why do we listen to God's word?

Jesus was a storyteller. He told stories about God's love. Sometimes his stories taught a lesson. Jesus wanted people to listen and to understand. Jesus wanted people to share the good news. His stories are in the Gospels. *Gospel* means "good news."

One day Jesus told a story about a sower. A sower is a person who puts seeds on the ground so they can grow.

Scripture

MATTHEW 13:1–23

The Sower

A sower went out to sow. As he sowed seed, some fell on the edge of the path and the birds ate them. Some fell on rocky ground. There was no soil there and the seed could not take root. The sun came up and burned it. Some seed fell among thorns. The thorns choked the seed and it could not grow. But some seed fell on good soil. These seeds grew and made much fruit.

The people did not understand the story. So Jesus explained it. He said that the seed on the path is like a person who hears God's word but does not understand it. The seed on the rocky ground is like the person who hears God's word but then forgets it. The seed that falls among the thorns is like the person who hears God's word but pays attention to other things and does not follow it. The seed that falls on good soil is like the person who hears God's word, understands it, and follows it.

BASED ON MATTHEW 13:1–23

❓ **What lesson did Jesus teach the people in his story?**

❓ **How do you follow God's word?**

Faith at Home

Read the scripture story with your child. Talk about ways you listen to God's word and follow it. Share one of your favorite scripture stories, and talk about what it means to each of you.

Share

Act it out   With a partner, choose one of the people Jesus was talking about in the story. Make up that scene from the Gospel story. Act out your part of the story for the rest of the group.

The Liturgy of the Word

SIGNS OF FAITH

The Readings

The reader reads the first and second readings from a book called the **lectionary**. The lectionary has all the Bible readings for every Sunday in it. The readings are read from a special place called the **ambo**. The Gospel is read from the **Book of the Gospels**, which is carried in procession during the Introductory Rites to show the importance of the four Gospels.

Faith Focus

What happens during the Liturgy of the Word?

The Mass has two very important parts. The first part is the **Liturgy of the Word**. The second part is the **Liturgy of the Eucharist**. In the Liturgy of the Word, we celebrate Jesus' presence in the word. In the Liturgy of the Eucharist, we celebrate Jesus' presence when we receive Holy Communion.

During the Liturgy of the Word, we listen to three readings from the Bible. Between the first two readings, we sing or pray a psalm. The psalm is a response, or answer, to God's word.

The first reading is usually from the Old Testament. The second reading is from the part of the New Testament that tells the story of the early followers of Jesus. The third reading is the Gospel. It tells the wonderful good news of Jesus. We greet the Gospel reading with joy. We say or sing "Alleluia!" *Alleluia* means "Praise the Lord."

Our Response

After the readings, the priest or deacon gives a homily. The homily helps us understand and follow God's word. The homily helps us understand how to live God's word. We respond to God's word when we stand and pray the Creed. We proudly profess what we believe.

Feasting on God's word makes us want to share with others who are hungry for good news. We close the Liturgy of the Word by praying together for the needs of the Church and all people around the world. These special prayers are called the general intercessions or prayer of the faithful.

❓ What do we call the part of the Mass when we listen to God's word?

Faith at Home

Talk with your child about how to listen attentively during the Liturgy of the Word. Encourage your child to pay special attention to the readings at Mass this Sunday. Then spend some time after Mass talking about how one of the readings or the homily relates to your family life.

Share God's Word

Respond

Draw a picture Show how you will share God's word at home or at school.

Closing Blessing

Gather and begin with the Sign of the Cross.

Leader: We praise and thank you, Lord, for the gift of your word.

All: Alleluia.

Leader: Help us to go forth and listen for your word in all we do. Show us how to speak your good news to others.

All: Amen.

 Sing together.

Open my ears, Lord.

Help me to hear your voice.

Open my ears, Lord.

Help me to hear.

LIVE

Faith at Home

Faith Focus

- The Bible is God's word written in human words.

- We listen to the word of God during the Liturgy of the Word.

- When we listen to God's word, we want to share it with others.

Ritual Focus

Signing   The celebration focused on listening to God's word. The children prayed by signing themselves with the Sign of the Cross on their forehead, lips, and heart. They prayed that God's word would be with them. At appropriate times during the week, pray the signing prayer on pages 32–33 with your child.

www.harcourtreligion.com
Visit our Web site for weekly scripture readings and questions, family resources, and more activities.

Act

Share Together   Using newspapers and magazines, cut out stories and pictures that show that God's word is alive today in people and events. Name some people who are in need of seeing God's word alive today. Create a family prayer of the faithful, and pray it this week during times you are together.

Do Together   Read Matthew 13:1–23, and talk about the question, "How can we bring the word of God to someone in need this week?" Check your parish bulletin for the names of those who might appreciate a get-well card or a card of encouragement. Have family members include their favorite verses.

Family Prayer

Jesus, bless us as we listen for your word this week. Open our eyes, our hearts, and minds that we will become more faithful followers and have the courage to spread your word to all those we meet. Amen.

We Gather

Procession

As you sing, walk forward slowly. Follow the person carrying the cross and Bible.

 Sing together.

> We praise you, O Lord
> For all your works are wonderful.
> We praise you, O Lord
> Forever is your love.
>
> © 1978 Damean Music

Leader: Let us pray.

> Make the Sign of the Cross together.

Ritual Focus: Honoring the Cross

Leader: God gives us many gifts. He gives us sun and rain. He gives us family and friends. He gives us our life. The most important gift God gives us is his Son, Jesus. Jesus shows us how to live. When Jesus died on the cross, he gave his life for all people. Let us think about what a wonderful gift Jesus gave us.

Sit silently.

Come forward, and put your hand on the cross.

We Listen

Leader: Gracious God, open our hearts to hear your word. We ask this through Jesus Christ our Lord.

All: Amen.

Leader: A reading from the holy Gospel according to John.

All: Glory to you, Lord.

Trace the Sign of the Cross on your forehead, lips, and heart.

Leader: Read John 13:1–16.

The Gospel of the Lord.

All: Praise to you, Lord Jesus Christ.

Sit silently.

Leader: Lord God, send us the Holy Spirit to show us how to live for others. We ask this in the name of Jesus, your Son.

All: Amen.

Leader: Let us pray as Jesus taught us:

Pray the Lord's Prayer together.

Let us offer each other the Sign of Peace.

Offer one another a sign of Christ's peace. Say: "The Peace of the Lord be with you." Answer: "And also with you."

We Go Forth

Leader: Loving God, send us out to share our lives with others. We ask this through Jesus Christ our Lord.

All: Amen.

 Sing the opening song together.

The Cross

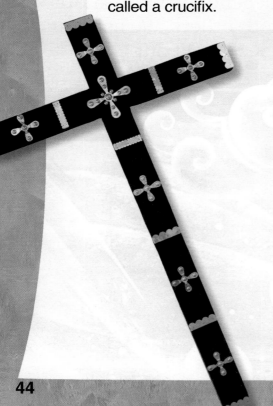

SIGNS OF FAITH

The Cross

The cross reminds us that Jesus gave his life for us. We see the cross in the church near the altar. Some Sundays the cross is carried in the Entrance Procession. On Good Friday we honor the cross in a special service. When a cross has a figure of Jesus on it, it is called a crucifix.

Reflect

Honoring the Cross   Think and write about the celebration.

When I think about all of God's gifts

_____

_____

_____

When I put my hand on the cross

_____

_____

When I think about Jesus

_____

_____

_____

Sacrifice

The cross reminds us that Jesus died for us. He died for our sins. He gave up his life as a sacrifice for all people. To *sacrifice* means to "give up something out of love for someone else." What a wonderful gift Jesus gave us—his life.

We sacrifice when we share with others. When we give up something to help someone, we sacrifice. We sacrifice out of love.

When the Church gathers for Mass, we remember the sacrifice of Jesus on the cross. The Mass is our sacrifice, too. At Mass we remember what we have done for God and others. We give God the gift of our lives.

SIGNS OF FAITH

The Altar

The **altar** is the central table in the front of the church. It is a sign of Jesus' presence with us. It is also a sign that the Mass is a sacrifice and a meal. Another name for the altar is "the Table of the Lord."

45

We Serve Others

Faith Focus

What does Jesus tell us about serving others?

On the night before he died, Jesus was at supper with his friends. He wanted to show his friends how much he loved them. He wanted to teach them how to show God's love to others.

JOHN 13:1–16

Scripture

The Washing of the Feet

Jesus was at the Last Supper with his disciples. He got up from the table. He took a towel and tied it around his waist. Then he poured water into a bowl. He began to wash the feet of the disciples.

The disciples were very surprised. Only servants washed feet! Jesus was not a servant. He was their Teacher.

Peter said to Jesus, "You will never wash my feet." Jesus said, "If you do not let me wash your feet, you cannot be my friend." Then Jesus washed the feet of all the disciples.

When he was finished, Jesus said, "Do you understand what I just did? You call me 'teacher' and 'master.' I am. If I have washed your feet, then you should wash one another's feet. What I do for you, you should do for others."

BASED ON JOHN 13:1–16

❓ **Why do you think Jesus washed his friends' feet?**

❓ **What does Jesus want you to do for others?**

Share

Write a story On a separate sheet of paper, make up a story about a child your age who makes a sacrifice for a brother, a sister, or a friend.

47

The Sacrifice of the Mass

SIGNS OF FAITH

Bread and Wine

Bread and wine are foods that people use for special meals. At Mass we use bread that is made without yeast. The wine comes from grapes. By the power of the Holy Spirit and the words and actions of the priest, the bread and wine become the Body and Blood of Jesus. They become our spiritual food.

Faith Focus

What gifts do we bring to the altar?

When Jesus washed the feet of the disciples, he showed us how to give our lives for others. Jesus gave his life for us on the cross. He saved us from our sins by his life, his death, and his Resurrection.

At Mass we remember Jesus' sacrifice during the Liturgy of the Eucharist. *Eucharist* means "thanksgiving." The Liturgy of the Eucharist is the second main part of the Mass. Through the power of the Holy Spirit and the words and actions of the priest, Jesus offers again the gift of himself to his Father.

During the Liturgy of the Eucharist, we thank God the Father for Jesus' sacrifice on the cross. We bring our lives and our sacrifices to the altar.

The sacrifices we make during the week are our gifts to God. They prepare us to join in Jesus' sacrifice.

Preparation of the Gifts

The Liturgy of the Eucharist begins with the Preparation of the Altar and the Gifts. Members of the assembly bring the bread and wine to the priest and they are placed on the altar.

We also offer gifts of money or other gifts. This offering is called a **collection**. These offerings help the parish do its work and take care of those in need. They are also a sign of our sacrifice.

The priest prepares the bread and wine and gives God thanks for his goodness.

We answer, "Blessed be God forever."

Then the priest prays that our sacrifice be acceptable to God.

We answer, "May the Lord accept the sacrifice at your hands for the praise and glory of his name, for our good, and the good of all his Church."

❓ **What gifts do you bring to Mass?**

49

I Serve Others

Respond

Color the cross In the spaces around the cross, write ways that you will serve others this week. Then color the cross.

Closing Blessing

Gather and begin with the Sign of the Cross.

Leader: God, our Father, we praise and thank you for the gift of your Son, Jesus.

All: Amen.

Leader: Jesus, our Savior, we praise and thank you for giving up your life for us.

All: Amen.

Sing together.

> We praise you, O Lord,
>
> For all your works are wonderful.
>
> We praise you, O Lord,
>
> Forever is your love.

Faith at Home

Faith Focus

- Jesus sacrificed his life for us when he died on the cross.

- The Mass is a sacrifice.

- At Mass, through the power of the Holy Spirit and the words and actions of the priest, Jesus offers again the gift of himself to his Father.

Ritual Focus

Honoring the Cross   The celebration focused on Honoring the Cross. The children reverenced the cross. Place a cross or crucifix in a place where the family gathers and says evening prayers.

Act

Share Together   Read John 13:1–16. Talk about what Jesus meant when he said, "What I do for you, you should do for others." Make a list of people who serve your family, such as sanitation workers, street crossing guards, doctors, or dentists. Discuss ways your family can thank these people for sharing their gifts.

Do Together   As a family, name some neighbors, family members, or friends who are in need of help or companionship, such as someone who is sick, lives alone, or needs to be tutored. Make a list of actions your family can take to serve these people sometime in the next month. Decide who will do what, and then mark it on the calendar.

Family Prayer

Gracious God, thank you for the gift of each other and especially for the gift of Jesus. Help us remain in your love and teach us to share it with others. Amen.

6 We Remember and Give Thanks

CELEBRATE

We Gather

Procession

As you sing, walk forward slowly. Follow the person carrying the Bible.

Te alabaré, Señor; tú me has librado.

I will praise you Lord; you have rescued me.

Tony Alonso © 2003 GIA Pub, Inc.

Leader: Let us pray.

Make the Sign of the Cross together.

We Listen

Leader: Loving Father, we come before you to remember and give thanks for your Son, Jesus. Open our hearts to the Holy Spirit to understand your word. We ask this through Jesus Christ our Lord.

All: Amen.

Leader: A reading from the holy Gospel according to Luke.

All: Glory to you, Lord.

Trace the Sign of the Cross on your forehead, lips, and heart.

Leader: Read Luke 22:14–20.

The Gospel of the Lord.

All: Praise to you, Lord Jesus Christ.

Sit silently.

Ritual Focus: Memorial Acclamation

Leader: Every time we gather together at the Eucharist, we know Jesus comes again to be with us. We are happy. We give God the Father thanks and praise for the mystery of Jesus' presence. We pray.

Kneel.

Let us proclaim the mystery of faith:

All: Christ has died.

Christ is risen.

Christ will come again.

Stand.

Leader: Let us pray as Jesus taught us:

Pray the Lord's Prayer together.

Leader: Let us offer each other the Sign of Peace.

Offer one another a sign of Christ's peace. Say: "The Peace of the Lord be with you." Answer: "And also with you."

We Go Forth

Leader: Loving Father, send us forth to bring Jesus' presence to one another. Help us to remember him. We ask this through Jesus Christ our Lord.

All: Amen.

Sing the opening song together.

We Remember

SIGNS OF FAITH

Kneeling

We kneel as a sign that we are God's children. When we kneel, we show we depend on God. Kneeling is one of the many ways we use our bodies to pray. Sometimes we kneel when we want to ask God for something. Other times we kneel when we seek God's forgiveness. At Mass we kneel after the Holy, Holy, Holy through the Great Amen. We also kneel during the Lamb of God before Holy Communion.

Reflect

Memorial Acclamation   Think and write about the celebration.

When I heard the story of the Last Supper

_____

_____

_____

When I knelt down

_____

_____

_____

When I prayed "Christ has died, Christ is risen, Christ will come again"

_____

_____

_____

The Eucharistic Prayer

The Eucharistic Prayer is the Church's great prayer of praise and thanksgiving to God. The priest begins this prayer. Together we pray, "Holy, Holy, Holy." Then we kneel as the prayer continues.

The priest prays to the Holy Spirit to make our gifts holy so they become the Body and Blood of Jesus. He retells the story of the Last Supper. We want to remember what Jesus did for us.

We proclaim the **mystery** of our faith. A mystery of faith is something we believe but we do not understand. We know that Jesus is with us now. We know that all people who love God will live with him in heaven when they die. We believe because Jesus promised us. We want to say, "Thank you."

SIGNS OF FAITH

The Priest

In the Eucharistic Prayer, we join our voices with all Catholics around the world. Jesus acts through the ministry of the priest. Only an ordained **priest** can lead the celebration of the Eucharist. This is the most important thing a priest does. Priests do many other things, too. They teach, preach, take care of the sick, and lead the parish.

Jesus Gives Thanks

Faith Focus

What does Jesus tell his friends?

Long ago, God led the people of Israel out of the land of Egypt where they had been slaves. He saved the people and set them free. Every year at the Passover meal, Jewish people remember and give thanks for God's saving love. They remember God's promises.

MATTHEW 26:26–28 AND LUKE 22:14–20

The Last Supper

On the night before he died, Jesus shared a special meal with his Apostles. They gathered to celebrate the Passover, a great Jewish holiday of thanksgiving.

We call this meal the Last Supper. During the meal, Jesus told his followers how to remember the mystery of our faith.

When it was time to begin, Jesus told his disciples that he had looked forward to eating the Passover meal with them. He knew he would soon suffer.

Jesus then used the bread and wine of the Passover in a new way. While they were eating, Jesus took bread. He said the blessing. He broke the bread. Then he gave the bread to the Apostles. He said, "Take and eat; this is my body."

Then Jesus took a cup of wine. Again he thanked God, his Father. He gave the cup to his disciples and said, "Drink from it. This is my blood, which will be shed for the forgiveness of sins. Do this in memory of me."

BASED ON MATTHEW 26:26–28 AND LUKE 22:14–20

❓ **What did Jesus and his disciples remember at the Passover?**

❓ **How do you remember Jesus?**

Faith at Home

Read the scripture story with your child. Discuss your child's responses to the questions. Talk about ways your family remembers important events, such as patriotic holidays, birthdays, and anniversaries.

Share

Write the message Look at the last paragraph in the story. In the space below, fill in the missing letters to spell Jesus' message.

Th__ __ __ __ m__ B__d__.

Th__ __ __ __ m__ Bl__ __d.

Reme__b__ __ __ __.

We Remember and Give Thanks

SIGNS OF FAITH

Blessed Sacrament

The consecrated Bread and Wine are the Body and Blood of Jesus. They are called the Blessed Sacrament. After Mass the remaining Hosts are placed in a special place called a **tabernacle**. The tabernacle is usually in a chapel or some other special place in the church. We keep the Blessed Sacrament there so it can be brought to parish members who are ill and cannot be present. We can also spend time before the tabernacle praying to Jesus in the Blessed Sacrament.

Faith Focus

What do we remember and give thanks for during the Eucharistic Prayer?

At the Last Supper, Jesus and the disciples remembered the Passover story. They said special prayers of thanks. We call the Eucharist "The Lord's Supper."

During the Eucharistic Prayer, the priest joins all of our prayers into one. He prays in our name and the name of the Church. We take part in the prayer, too. During the prayer, we remember all the ways that God has saved us. We offer ourselves to God with Jesus. We share in Jesus' dying and rising through the power of the Holy Spirit. We remember and we say, "Thank you."

The priest asks God to accept our sacrifice. We pray that God will make us holy, like the saints who are in heaven with him. We pray for one another. We offer the Mass for the people who have died.

Consecration

An important part of the Eucharistic Prayer is the **consecration**. The priest says the words Jesus did at the Last Supper. Through the power of the Holy Spirit and the words and actions of the priest, the gifts of bread and wine become the Body and Blood of Christ.

After the consecration we remember that Jesus gave his life for us. The priest says or sings: "Let us proclaim the mystery of faith." We answer with a special response. This response is the Memorial Acclamation.

The Great Amen

At the end of the Eucharistic Prayer, the priest prays the prayer that begins,

"Through him, with him, and in him."

We answer, "Amen."

This response is the Great Amen. We say "yes" to God's promises. We praise him for his gifts and saving actions.

❓ **How is the Eucharist like the Last Supper?**

Faith at Home

Review your child's response to the question. Go over the meaning of the word *Amen*. Go through the Eucharistic Prayer on these pages with your child. Familiarize your child with the responses to the prayer.

Say "Yes"

Respond

Make a stained glass window   In the picture below, color the spaces with an "a" yellow. Color the spaces with a "b" red. Choose another color to fill in the areas marked with "c" to complete the stained-glass window. Then write one way you can say "yes" to Jesus this week.

_____

Closing Blessing

Gather and begin with the Sign of the Cross.

Leader: God, our Father, we remember and give thanks for all your good gifts.

All: Amen.

Leader: Jesus, our Savior, we remember and give thanks for your death and Resurrection.

All: Amen.

Leader: Holy Spirit, we remember and give thanks that you are with us.

All: Amen.

🎼 Sing together.

Te alabaré, Señor; tú me has librado.

I will praise you Lord; you have rescued me.

Tony Alonso © 2003 GIA Pub, Inc.

Faith at Home

Faith Focus

- The Eucharistic Prayer is a prayer of thanksgiving, remembering, and consecration.

- Through the power of the Holy Spirit and the words and actions of the priest, the bread and wine become the Body and Blood of Jesus.

- At the Great Amen, the assembly says "yes" to all of God's saving actions and promises.

Ritual Focus

Memorial Acclamation   The celebration focused on the Memorial Acclamation. The children prayed the Acclamation. During the week, use the Family Prayer as a prayer before or after meals.

www.harcourtreligion.com
Visit our Web site for weekly scripture readings and questions, family resources, and more activities.

Act

Share Together   Talk about ways your family remembers people who have moved away or died. Use examples of pictures or stories to get the sharing started. Make a list of the examples that family members share. Use the list to talk about ways your family can remember Jesus during the week.

Do Together   Plan a time to make a visit to the Blessed Sacrament with your child. Your parish church may have a Blessed Sacrament chapel set apart from the body of the church. Go near the place where the tabernacle is located. Spend some quiet time in conversation with Jesus in the Blessed Sacrament.

Family Prayer

Giving God, we give you thanks for all the gifts you give us: for the gifts of creation, for family and friends, and especially for the gift of your Son, Jesus. Help us to always remember that you are here with us. Amen.

Chapter 7

We Share a Meal

We Gather

Procession

As you sing, walk forward slowly. Follow the person carrying the Bible. Gather around the table.

 Sing together.

> We come to the Table of the Lord
> As one body formed in your love.
> We come to the Table of the Lord
> As one body formed in your love.

© 2004 John Burland

Leader: Let us pray.

Make the Sign of the Cross together.

We Listen

Leader: God, our Father, you provide us with everything we need. Strengthen us to bring life to others. We ask this through Jesus Christ our Lord.

All: Amen.

Leader: A reading from the holy Gospel according to John.

All: Glory to you, Lord.

Trace the Sign of the Cross on your forehead, lips, and heart.

Leader: Read John 6:30–58.

The Gospel of the Lord.

All: Praise to you, Lord Jesus Christ.

Sit silently.

Ritual Focus: Sharing a Meal

Be seated around the table.

Leader: Blessed are you, almighty
Father,

who gives us our daily bread.

Blessed is your only begotten
Son,

who continually feeds us
with the word of life.

Blessed is the Holy Spirit,

who brings us together at
this table of love.

Blessed be God now and
for ever.

All: Amen.

BOOK OF BLESSINGS, 1069

Share the food at the table.

Leader: We give you thanks for all
your gifts, almighty God,
living and reigning now and
for ever.

All: Amen.

BOOK OF BLESSINGS, 1070

We Go Forth

Leader: Loving God, we thank you for
food, for families, for friends, and
for the gift of your Son, Jesus.
Help us to share the gifts of life
with others. We ask this in the
name of your Son, Jesus.

All: Amen.

 Sing the opening song together.

Special Meals

SIGNS OF FAITH

Sign of Peace

During Mass we offer one another the **Sign of Peace** before Holy Communion. The Sign of Peace is an action prayer. We reach out our hand to people around us. We wish them God's peace. Giving the Sign of Peace to others is a sign that we are united to one another at the Table of the Lord.

Reflect

Sharing a meal   Think and write about the celebration.

I like sharing meals with others because

_____

_____

_____

When I eat good food

_____

_____

_____

Bread reminds me of

_____

_____

_____

The Eucharist as a Meal

Sharing a meal brings people closer together. A special meal, sometimes called a banquet or feast, is a time to celebrate. It is a time to share stories, sing songs, and eat special food. When families and friends gather for special meals, they grow in love.

The Eucharist is the Church's special meal. The Holy Spirit gathers us with our parish family and with Catholics all over the world. We gather at the Eucharist to celebrate God's love for us. We also share Jesus' own Body and Blood in Holy Communion. Jesus is truly present in both the consecrated Bread and the Wine.

Jesus is the Bread of Life. In the meal of the Eucharist, we share in the life of the Risen Christ.

SIGNS OF FAITH

Paten, Ciborium, and Chalice
The food for our Eucharistic meal is placed on special dishes. The **paten** holds the hosts. Sometimes a **ciborium** may be used as well. The wine is poured into a **chalice**.

We Share the Bread of Life

Faith Focus

What does Jesus tell us about himself?

Jesus shared many meals with people. One time, Jesus was talking to a large crowd at dinnertime. He saw that people were hungry, and he fed them with only five loaves of bread and a few fish. The people were amazed!

Scripture

JOHN 6:30–58

I Am the Bread of Life

When the people saw Jesus feed so many with so little food, they wanted him to perform more miracles. "You are like Moses," they said. "When the people of Israel were hungry in the desert, Moses gave them manna, bread from heaven." But Jesus reminded them that it was God the Father, not Moses, who gave food to the people. Then he taught the people a very important lesson about himself.

"My Father sent me to bring you life that lasts forever. I myself am the bread of life; whoever comes to me will never be hungry. No one who believes in me will ever be thirsty."

Jesus continued, "I am the bread from heaven. The people who ate manna in the desert eventually died, as all humans die. But if you share my own flesh and blood, I will always be with you. You will live forever with God."

"What is he talking about?" some people asked. Jesus answered them, "Whoever shares in my life will live forever. Just as the Father sent me and I have life because of him, so too will the one who eats the Bread of Life have life."

BASED ON JOHN 6:30–58

❓ **What do you think Jesus means when he says he is the Bread of Life?**

❓ **How can you share in Jesus' life?**

Faith at Home

Read the scripture story with your child. Make connections between the effects of food for our physical bodies and Jesus as the food for our spirit. Together, decide on one activity you can do this week to remember that Jesus is the Bread of Life.

Share

Draw a picture Draw one way Jesus gives you what you need to live.

The Communion Rite

SIGNS OF FAITH

Lamb of God

The **Lamb of God** is a title for Jesus. This title reminds us that Jesus gave up his life for our sins. When we pray or sing this prayer before Holy Communion, we remember that through Jesus' death and Resurrection our sins are forgiven and we have peace.

Faith Focus

What happens during the Communion Rite?

We receive Jesus, the Bread of Life, in Holy Communion. What does this mean?

- We are united to Jesus.

- Our friendship with Jesus grows stronger.

- God forgives our less serious sins if we are sorry and gives us strength to avoid serious sin.

- We are united with the whole Church, the Body of Christ.

- We share in God's promise that we will live in heaven with Jesus, Mary, and all the saints.

We prepare ourselves to receive Holy Communion. Together we stand and pray the Lord's Prayer. We remember we are one family with God. As a sign of unity, we share the Sign of Peace with each other.

Holy Communion

During Holy Communion, the priest invites us to the table. He reminds us of Jesus' sacrifice and presence in the Eucharist. He holds up the large Host and says, "This is the Lamb of God, who takes away the sins of the world. Happy are those who are called to his supper." We come forward in a procession. Sometimes we sing.

When it is our turn to receive Jesus, we cup our hands with one hand on top of the other. The priest, deacon, or extraordinary minister of Holy Communion says, "The body of Christ." We answer, "Amen."

Often, we may also receive from the cup. After we swallow the Host, we go to the deacon or extraordinary minister of Holy Communion, who offers the cup and says, "The blood of Christ." We answer, "Amen." We return to our places. We pray or sing a prayer of thanksgiving.

We should receive Holy Communion every time we participate in the Mass. We must do so at least once a year.

❓ **Why are we happy to share in the Lord's Supper?**

Faith at Home

Review your child's response to the question. Talk about what happens when we receive Holy Communion by referring to the list on page 68. Use this page to show your child how to go to Holy Communion.

Receive Jesus

Respond

Write a prayer   In the space below, write a prayer. Share your thoughts and feelings about receiving Jesus for the first time in Holy Communion.

_____

_____

_____

_____

_____

_____

_____

Closing Blessing

Gather and begin with the Sign of the Cross.

Leader: God, our Father, we praise and thank you for the gift of life.

All: Amen.

Leader: Jesus, our Savior, we praise and thank you for giving yourself to us in Holy Communion.

All: Amen.

Leader: Holy Spirit, giver of God's gifts, we praise and thank you for helping us live as members of the Body of Christ.

All: Amen.

Sing together.

We come to the Table of the Lord

As one body formed in your love.

We come to the Table of the Lord

As one body formed in your love.

© 2004 John Burland

Faith at Home

Faith Focus

- The Mass is a meal of thanksgiving.

- Jesus is the Bread of Life.

- In Holy Communion we are united to Jesus and the Church. We share in the promise of life forever with God.

Ritual Focus

Sharing a Meal   The celebration focused on Sharing a Meal. The children prayed a blessing prayer and shared food. During the week, use the Blessing Prayer on page 63 as the prayer before your main meal.

www.harcourtreligion.com
Visit our Web site for weekly scripture readings and questions, family resources, and more activities.

Act

Share Together   As a family, share a special meal of remembering and celebration. Encourage each member to bring pictures, symbols, or souvenirs of his or her favorite time as a family. Share the memories during the meal, and end the meal with a family prayer.

Do Together   As a family, prepare a meal for an elderly couple or a family where a parent is sick or a new baby has arrived. Plan the meal, contact the family to choose a convenient time, prepare the meal, and deliver it. As an option, volunteer to serve meals at a soup kitchen or Catholic Worker house.

Family Prayer

Lord, thank you for all the gifts you have given us. Thank you for family and friends. Help us grow strong in love for one another and for you. Send us the Holy Spirit to show us how to share your life and love with others. Amen.

8 We Go Forth

CELEBRATE

We Gather

Procession

As you sing, walk forward slowly. Follow the person carrying the Bible.

 Sing together.

> Go now, love each other.
>
> Thanks be to God.
>
> We will be your spirit.
>
> We will be your peace.
>
> Let us love each other.
>
> Lead us to the feast.

© 1998 Tom Kendzia, OCP

Leader: Let us pray.

Make the Sign of the Cross together.

We Listen

Leader: Loving God, open our hearts to the Holy Spirit as we listen to your word. We ask this through Jesus Christ our Lord.

All: Amen.

Leader: A reading from the Acts of the Apostles.

Read Acts 2:1–41.

The word of the Lord.

All: Thanks be to God.

Sit silently.

Ritual Focus: Blessing for Mission

Come forward, and gather around the holy water.

Leader: Just as the disciples were filled with the Holy Spirit and told the good news in word and action, so are we. Let us pray for God's blessing.

Lord Jesus, you came on earth to serve others. May your example strengthen us.

All: Amen.

Leader: Through your dying and rising, you made a new world where we are called to love one another. May we live according to your Gospel.

All: Amen.

Leader: Let us pray that God, who is love, will light our hearts with the fire of the Holy Spirit.

Bow your heads, and pray for God's blessing.

Blessed are you, God of mercy. Through your Son Jesus, you gave us an example of love. Send down your blessing on your children. Let them serve you in their neighbor.

All: Amen.

ADAPTED FROM THE BOOK OF BLESSINGS, 587

We Go Forth

Make the Sign of the Cross with the water.

Leader: Go forth now to love and serve the Lord.

All: Thanks be to God.

 Sing the opening song together.

Being Blessed

SIGNS OF FAITH

Blessing

A blessing is an action, using words and gestures, to ask God to show his kindness to us. There are many kinds of blessings. The Church blesses people and objects. Parents are blessed when their children are baptized. Animals are blessed on the feast of Saint Francis. Parents bless children at night or when they wake in the morning. The priest blesses special objects such as rosaries. At Mass the priest blesses the assembly.

Reflect

Blessing for a mission Think and write about the celebration.

When I receive a blessing

_____

_____

_____

The Holy Spirit helps me

_____

_____

_____

When I serve people in need

_____

_____

_____

Sent on a Mission

Have you ever been sent to do a special job? Being sent means you are trusted. You represent someone else. You are responsible. Someone is counting on you. Without you, the job will not get done.

At the end of Mass, we are sent to carry the message of God's love to others. We are sent to help carry out the work of Jesus in the world. The word *Mass* comes from a word that means "to be sent on a mission." Receiving Jesus in Holy Communion strengthens us to love and serve others. We go out from Mass with God's blessing.

SIGNS OF FAITH

Witness

At the end of Mass, we are sent forth to be witnesses of faith in Jesus' presence in the world today. A witness is somebody who sees or hears something and tells others about it. We witness to Jesus' presence when we tell others about him in our words and in our actions.

The Holy Spirit

Faith Focus

What happens when we receive the Holy Spirit?

Before Jesus returned to his Father in heaven, he gave his disciples a mission. He wanted them to teach others about his message. Jesus promised the disciples he would send the Holy Spirit to help them with their mission. Fifty days after Jesus' Resurrection, his promise came true.

Scripture

ACTS 2:1–41

Pentecost

During the feast of Pentecost, the disciples were all in one place together. Suddenly there came from the sky a noise like a strong wind. It filled the whole house. Then flames of fire came to rest above each of the disciples' heads. The disciples were filled with the Holy Spirit. They went out into the street and began to tell the crowd about Jesus and his message. The people who listened were surprised because the disciples were speaking in different languages. They wondered if something was wrong with the disciples!

Peter raised his voice and said, "There is nothing wrong with us. What has happened is the work of the Holy Spirit. Jesus of Nazareth has sent the Holy Spirit as he promised." Then Peter said, "This Jesus whom you crucified has been raised from the dead. He is the Messiah."

The people wanted to believe. They said, "What shall we do?" Peter told them, "Turn to God and be baptized, in the name of Jesus Christ. Your sins will be forgiven and you will receive the Holy Spirit." About three thousand people were baptized that day.

BASED ON ACTS 2:1–41

❓ **What did the Holy Spirit do for the disciples?**

❓ **How does the Holy Spirit help you?**

Faith at Home

Read the scripture story with your child. Discuss your child's responses to the questions. Share times when you call on the Holy Spirit for help. Review the Prayer to the Holy Spirit on pages 72–73. Choose an appropriate time each day to pray the prayer together—for example, before meals, at bedtime, or in the car.

Share

Write a rhyme On a separate sheet of paper, write your own rhyme about the Holy Spirit. Use at least three of the words below.

Holy Spirit	play	wide
in	be	guide
today	pray	help

We Are Sent

Deacon

A **deacon** is a man ordained by the bishop to do works of charity and to have a special role in worship. Some deacons become priests. Other deacons do not, but they help the bishop and care for people who need it. All deacons can baptize and witness a marriage. At Mass deacons may carry the Book of the Gospels, read the Gospel, and preach. They can also send us forth for mission at the end of Mass.

Faith Focus

How do we love and serve Jesus?

Like Peter and the disciples, Jesus promises us the Holy Spirit. The Holy Spirit is with us always. The Holy Spirit helps us:

- tell others about his love
- do the work of being a disciple
- forgive others
- care about people who need help, especially those who are poor

HAPPY ANNIVERSARY

Go Forth

At the end of Mass, we are sent forth to serve others. The priest or deacon says, "Go in peace to love and serve the Lord." We respond, "Thanks be to God." We go forth to share the joyful good news that Jesus is alive. We share the good news by what we say and what we do.

When we leave the church after Mass, we are different from when we came in. Participating in the Eucharist changes us. It brings us closer to God the Father, Son, and Holy Spirit. It also brings us closer to one another.

In the Eucharist we become one body, just as many grains of wheat make one loaf of bread. We are filled with God's grace and love. We go forth to serve others. We go forth to help those who need our help. We love and serve Jesus when we love and serve one another.

❓ **What are some ways your family helps others?**

Sent to Serve

Respond

Write a story Write a story about how you can serve others.

_____

_____

_____

_____

_____

_____

_____

Closing Blessing

Gather and begin with the Sign of the Cross.

Leader: God, our Father, send us forth to tell the world about your love.

All: Amen.

Leader: Jesus, our Savior, send us forth to serve others.

All: Amen.

Leader: Holy Spirit, guide us to see the places where we are called to love and serve.

All: Amen.

 Sing together.

Go now, love each other.

Thanks be to God.

We will be your spirit.

We will be your peace.

Let us love each other.

Lead us to the feast.

LIVE

Faith at Home

Faith Focus

- The Eucharist changes us.
- The Holy Spirit helps us to live out our mission.
- At Mass we are sent forth to love and serve others.

Ritual Focus

Blessing for Mission The celebration focused on being sent forth for mission. The children were blessed and sent forth. Establish a family ritual of blessing each other with the Sign of the Cross on the forehead when you leave the house in the morning.

www.harcourtreligion.com
Visit our Web site for weekly scripture readings and questions, family resources, and more activities.

Act

Share Together Make a list of ways members of your family show love and care for each other. Then brainstorm together other ways the family might continue to show love and care. Suggest a family "love and serve" week. Write the names of family members on separate slips of paper. Have each member draw a name. Invite family members to do some "love and serve" actions for that person.

Do Together Obtain copies of the parish bulletin or newsletter. As a family, go through it and locate parish activities of service and outreach. Choose one that the whole family can get involved in, and call the parish to volunteer. After volunteering, hold a family discussion about the experience and how it felt to love and serve others.

Love and Serve Week

Family Prayer

Come Holy Spirit, show us the way and give us the strength to love and serve others. Amen.

Catholic Source Book

Words of Faith

Altar The table of the Eucharist. The Liturgy of the Eucharist is celebrated at the altar.

Altar Server A person who helps the priest and deacon at Mass.

Ambo The reading stand from which the Scriptures are proclaimed. It is sometimes called the lectern.

Assembly The baptized community gathered to celebrate the Eucharist, the sacraments, or other liturgy.

Baptism One of the three Sacraments of Initiation. Baptism gives us new life in God and makes us members of the Church.

Baptismal Font A bowl-shaped container or pool of water used for Baptism. The word *font* means "fountain."

Bible God's word written in human words. The Bible is the holy book of the Church.

Blessed Sacrament Another name for the Body and Blood of Jesus.

Blessing An action using words and gestures which asks God to show his kindness to us.

Body of Christ A name for the Church. It tells us that Christ is the head and the baptized are the members of the body.

 **Book of the Gospels** A decorated book containing the readings from the four Gospels used during the Liturgy of the Word.

Cantor The leader of song during the Mass and other Church celebrations.

 **Chalice** The special silver or gold cup used at Mass to hold the wine that becomes the Blood of Christ.

Chrism The oil blessed by the bishop used in the Sacraments of Baptism, Confirmation, and Holy Orders.

Christian The name given to people who are baptized and follow Jesus.

Church The community of all baptized people who believe in God and follow Jesus.

 **Ciborium** The special silver or gold container used at Mass to hold the smaller consecrated Hosts for communion. A covered ciborium also holds the Blessed Sacrament in the tabernacle.

Collection The gifts of money collected from members of the assembly and presented during the time of the Preparation of the Altar.

 **Confirmation** One of the three Sacraments of Initiation. It is the sacrament that strengthens the life of God we received at Baptism and seals us with the gift of the Holy Spirit.

Confiteor A prayer of sorrow for sin. In it each person tells God and the Church family, "I am sorry." We ask for forgiveness.

Consecration The part of the Eucharistic Prayer when, through the prayers and actions of the priest and the power of the Holy Spirit, the gifts of bread and wine become the Body and Blood of Jesus.

Cruets Small pitchers or containers that hold the water and wine used at Mass.

Deacon A man who is ordained to serve the Church. Deacons may baptize, proclaim the Gospel, preach, assist the priest at Mass, witness marriages, and do works of charity.

Eucharist One of the three Sacraments of Initiation. It is the sacrament of the Body and Blood of Christ. Jesus is truly and really present in the Eucharist. The word *Eucharist* means "thanksgiving."

Grace A sharing in God's own life.

Holy Communion The Body and Blood of Christ that we receive in the Eucharist.

Holy Trinity The three Persons in one God: God the Father, God the Son, and God the Holy Spirit.

Host A round piece of unleavened bread used at Mass. When the host is consecrated at Mass, it becomes the Body and Blood of Christ.

Incense Oils and spices that are burned in liturgical celebrations to show honor for holy things. It is also used as a sign of our prayers rising to God.

Lamb of God   A title for Jesus that reminds us that he offered his life through suffering and death to take away our sins.

Lectionary   The book of scripture readings used at Mass.

Lector   A person who proclaims God's word at Mass or other liturgical celebrations. The word *lector* means "reader."

Liturgy of the Eucharist   The second main part of the Mass. It is the time when we call on the Holy Spirit and the priest consecrates the bread and wine. We remember and give thanks for all of God's gifts, especially Jesus' life, death, and Resurrection.

Liturgy of the Word   The first main part of the Mass. It is the time when we listen to God's word in the Scriptures.

Mass   Another name for the Eucharist.

Memorial   Another word for remembering. In the Mass, it means to remember and proclaim God's works.

Mission   A job or duty someone is sent to do and takes responsibility for. The Church's mission is to announce the good news of God's kingdom.

Mystery   Something we believe about God and his actions, but we do not understand how it happens.

Original Sin   The first sin committed by the first humans.

Paschal candle Another name for the Easter Candle that is lit at the Easter Vigil.

paten The silver or gold plate or dish used at Mass to hold the large host.

Pentecost The feast that celebrates the coming of the Holy Spirit on the Apostles and disciples fifty days after Easter. We celebrate this day as the beginning of the Church.

People of God A name for the Church which tells us that we are sent by Christ to preach God's love to all people.

prayer Talking and listening to God. It is raising our minds and hearts to God.

preparation of the altar and gifts The part of the Mass when the altar is prepared and members of the assembly bring the bread and wine, which will become the Body and Blood of Jesus, to the priest at the altar.

priest A man who is ordained to serve God and lead the Church by celebrating the sacraments, preaching and presiding at Mass, and performing other spiritual works.

procession A group of people moving forward as part of a celebration.

sacrament An outward sign that comes from Jesus, which gives us a share in God's life.

sacramentary The book containing the Order of the Mass, special celebrations during the year, and various prayers used by the priest at Mass.

Sacraments of Initiation The three Sacraments of Baptism, Confirmation, and Holy Eucharist that together make us full members of the Church. They are signs that we belong to God and to the Catholic Church.

Sanctuary   The part of the church where the altar and ambo are located. The word *sanctuary* means "holy place."

Sign of Peace   The sign of peace is an action prayer that we exchange before Communion as a sign to wish God's peace on those who receive it. It shows that we are one in Christ's love.

Tabernacle   The container in which the Blessed Sacrament is kept. It may be located in the sanctuary or a special chapel in the church. A lamp or candle is kept burning near the tabernacle as a sign that Jesus is present. The word *tabernacle* means "meeting place."

Unity   A word that means to be one with others.

Usher   A person of hospitality who welcomes members of the assembly to Mass and helps direct processions and collections.

Vestments   The special clothing worn by the priest and some others for Mass and other liturgical celebrations.

Order of the Mass

Every Sunday we gather together united as one with all the members of the Church to give praise and thanks to God.

Introductory Rites

During the Introductory Rites, we prepare to listen to God's word and prepare to celebrate the Eucharist.

Entrance

The priest, deacon, and other ministers begin the procession to the altar. We stand and sing. The Greeting and our response shows that we are gathered together as the Church.

Greeting of the Altar and the People

When the procession reaches the altar, the priest, deacon, and other ministers make a profound bow. The priest and deacon also kiss the altar as a sign of reverence. At special times the priest will burn incense at the cross and altar. The priest goes to his chair and leads us in the Sign of the Cross and Greeting.

Priest: In the name of the Father, and of the Son, and of the Holy Spirit.

People: Amen.

Priest: The grace and peace of God our Father and the Lord Jesus Christ be with you.

People: And also with you.

Rite of Sprinkling with Holy Water

On some Sundays, the priest does a Rite of Sprinkling in place of the Penitential Rite. We are blessed with holy water to remind us of our Baptism.

Penitential Rite

The priest invites the assembly to confess our sins together.

Confiteor

I confess to Almighty God
and to you, my brothers and sisters,
that I have sinned through my own fault,
in my thoughts and in my words,
in what I have done,
and in what I have failed to do;
and I ask Blessed Mary ever virgin,
all the angels and saints,
and you, my brothers and sisters,
to pray for me to the Lord our God.

Lord Have Mercy

Priest: Lord, have mercy.

People: Lord, have mercy.

Priest: Christ, have mercy.

People: Christ, have mercy.

Priest: Lord, have mercy.

People: Lord, have mercy.

Priest: May almighty God have mercy on us, forgive us our sins, and bring us to everlasting life.

People: Amen.

Gloria

On some Sundays, we praise God the Father, the Son, and the Holy Spirit.

Glory to God in the highest,
and peace to his people on earth.
Lord God, heavenly King,
almighty God and Father,
we worship you, we give you thanks,
we praise you for your glory.
Lord Jesus Christ, only Son of the Father,
Lord God, Lamb of God,
you take away the sin of the world:
have mercy on us;
you are seated at the right hand of the Father:
receive our prayer.
For you alone are the Holy One,
you alone are the Lord,
you alone are the Most High,
Jesus Christ,
with the Holy Spirit,
in the glory of God the Father. Amen.

Collect

The priest invites us to pray. We are silent for a moment and remember we are in God's presence. We think about what we want to pray for.

Priest: Let us pray…
People: Amen.

Liturgy of the Word

The Liturgy of the Word is celebrated at every Mass. We listen to God's word in the Readings and Homily, and we respond to God's word in the Creed and Prayers of the Faithful. The lectors and the priest or deacon read the readings from the ambo.

First Reading

We sit and listen to God's word from the Old Testament or the Acts of the Apostles. At the end of the reading, we respond:

Reader: The word of the Lord.
People: Thanks be to God.

Responsorial Psalm

At the end of the first reading, the cantor, or song leader, leads us in singing a psalm from the Old Testament.

People: Sing or say the refrain.

Second Reading

We listen to God's word from the New Testament books that are not Gospels. At the end of the reading, we respond:

Reader: The word of the Lord.
People: Thanks be to God.

Acclamation Before the Gospel

We stand and welcome the Lord, who speaks to us in the Gospel reading. We sing an Alleluia or another acclamation to profess our faith in God's presence.

People: Sing or say the Alleluia or Gospel Acclamation.

Gospel

Priest or deacon: The Lord be with you.

People: And also with you.

Priest or deacon: A reading from the holy Gospel according to...

People: Glory to you, Lord.

The priest and people make the Sign of the Cross on the forehead, lips, and heart.

At the end of the Gospel, we respond:

Priest or deacon: The Gospel of the Lord.

People: Praise to you, Lord Jesus Christ.

Homily

We sit and listen. The priest or deacon helps us understand the word of God. He shows us how we can live as Jesus' disciples.

Profession of Faith

We stand and respond to the readings by saying the Creed. We profess our faith in God the Father, God the Son, and God the Holy Spirit. We pray the Nicene Creed or the Apostles' Creed.

(For Nicene Creed, see page 92. For Apostles' Creed, see page 102.)

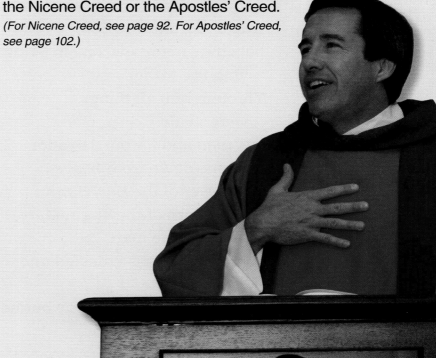

Nicene Creed

People: We believe in one God, the Father,
the Almighty,
maker of heaven and earth,
of all that is seen and unseen.
We believe in one Lord,
Jesus Christ,
the only Son of God,
eternally begotten of the Father,
God from God, Light from Light,
true God from true God,
begotten, not made, one in Being
with the Father.
Through him all things
were made.
For us men and for our salvation
he came down from heaven:
by the power of the Holy Spirit
he was born of the Virgin Mary,
and became man.
For our sake he was crucified under
Pontius Pilate;
he suffered, died, and was buried.

On the third day he rose
again in fulfillment of
the Scriptures;
he ascended into heaven and is
seated at the right hand of
the Father.
He will come again in glory
to judge the living and the dead,
and his kingdom will have
no end.
We believe in the Holy Spirit, the
Lord, the giver of life,
who proceeds from the Father
and the Son.
With the Father and the Son he is
worshiped and glorified.
He has spoken through the
Prophets.
We believe in one holy
catholic and apostolic Church.
We acknowledge one baptism for
the forgiveness of sins.
We look for the resurrection of the
dead, and the life of the world
to come.
Amen.

General Intercessions

We stand and the priest, deacon, or a layperson leads us in praying for the needs of the Church, the world, those who need our prayers, and our local community. We say or sing the response that the leader tells us to say or sing.

Liturgy of the Eucharist

During the Liturgy of the Eucharist, we bring our gifts of bread and wine to the altar. We give thanks to God the Father for all the ways he has saved us. Our gifts of bread and wine become the Body and Blood of Christ. We all receive the Lord's Body and the Lord's Blood in communion.

Preparation of the Gifts

We sit as the gifts of bread and wine are brought to the altar. The altar is prepared as the collection is taken up. Sometimes we sing a song during the preparation.

The priest lifts up the bread and prays:

Priest: Blessed are you, Lord God of all creation.
Through your goodness we have this bread to offer which earth has given and human hands have made. It will become for us the bread of life.

People: Blessed be God forever.

The priest lifts up the chalice of wine and prays:

Priest: Blessed are you, Lord God of all creation.
Through your goodness we have this wine to offer, fruit of the vine and work of human hands.
It will become our spiritual drink.

People: Blessed be God forever.

The priest calls us to pray.

Priest: Pray, my brothers and sisters, that our sacrifice may be acceptable to God, the almighty Father.

People: May the Lord accept the sacrifice at your hands
for the praise and glory of his name,
for our good,
and the good of all his Church.

Prayer over the Offerings

We stand and pray with the priest. We prepare for the Eucharistic Prayer.

People: Amen.

Eucharistic Prayer

This is the central prayer of the Eucharist. It is a prayer of thanksgiving and making holy.

Preface

The priest invites us to pray. We say or sing the preface.

Priest: The Lord be with you.

People: And also with you.

Priest: Lift up your hearts.

People: We lift them up to the Lord.

Priest: Let us give thanks to the Lord our God.

People: It is right to give him thanks and praise.

Acclamation

Together with the priest, we say or sing:

Holy, holy, holy Lord, God of power
and might,
Heaven and earth are full of your glory.
Hosanna in the Highest.
Blessed is he who comes in the name
of the Lord.
Hosanna in the highest.

The priest continues to pray the Eucharistic prayer. During the Eucharistic prayer the priest tells the story of all of God's saving actions.

Consecration

The priest takes the bread and says the words of Jesus:

Take this, all of you, and eat it:
this is my Body which will be given up
for you.

The priest holds up the consecrated bread, the Host, which is now the Body of Christ.

Then the priest takes the chalice, the cup of wine, and says the words of Jesus:

Take this, all of you, and drink from it:
this is the cup of my Blood,
the Blood of the new and everlasting
  covenant.
It will be shed for you and for all
so that sins may be forgiven.
Do this in memory of me.

The bread and wine become the Body and Blood of Jesus through the power of the Holy Spirit and the words and actions of the priest. Jesus is truly present under the appearances of bread and wine. We proclaim our faith in Jesus.

Memorial Acclamation

**Priest or
deacon:** Let us proclaim the mystery
of faith.

People: Christ has died, Christ is risen,
Christ will come again.

The priest continues the Eucharistic Prayer. He prays for the whole Church, those who are living and those who are dead. He ends the prayer by singing or saying aloud:

Priest: Through him, with him, in him,
in the unity of the Holy Spirit,
all glory and honor is yours,
almighty Father, for ever and ever.

People: Amen.

Communion Rite

We stand for the Lord's Prayer. We pray for our daily bread. We pray our sins will be forgiven.

Lord's Prayer

People: Our Father, who art in heaven,
hallowed be thy name;
thy kingdom come;
thy will be done on earth as it is in
heaven.
Give us this day our daily bread;
and forgive us our trespasses
as we forgive those who trespass
against us;
and lead us not into temptation,
But deliver us from evil.

Priest: Deliver us, Lord, from every evil…

People: For the kingdom, the power
and the glory are yours,
now and forever.

Sign of Peace

The priest or deacon invites us to share a Sign of Peace with those around us. We pray for peace and that the Church and the world will be united as one.

Priest: The peace of the Lord be with you always.

People: And also with you.

We offer one another a sign of peace.

Breaking of the Bread

Just as Jesus broke bread at the Last Supper and gave it to his disciples, the priest breaks the consecrated bread and puts a piece of it into the chalice to show the unity of Jesus' Body and Blood. During the breaking of the bread, we say or sing:

People: Lamb of God, you take away the sins of the world: have mercy on us. Lamb of God, you take away the sins of the world: have mercy on us. Lamb of God, you take away the sins of the world: grant us peace.

Communion

The priest shows us the consecrated bread. He holds the Host up and invites us to the banquet of the Lord. We respond:

People: Lord, I am not worthy to receive you, but only say the word and I shall be healed.

The priest receives Holy Communion. We sing the Communion hymn. When it is time, we walk in procession to receive Holy Communion. The minister offers us the consecrated bread, the Body of Christ. We bow our heads as a sign of reverence before receiving the Body of Christ.

Priest or extraordinary minister: The Body of Christ.

People: Amen.

We receive the Body of Christ in our hand or on our tongue. We reverently chew and swallow the consecrated bread.

If we are receiving the consecrated wine, the Blood of Christ, the minister offers us the cup. We bow our head as a sign of reverence before receiving the Blood of Christ.

> **Priest or extraordinary minister:** The Blood of Christ.
> **People:** Amen.

We return to our seats and give thanks for the wonderful gift of Jesus we have received in Communion.

When the distribution of Communion is finished, the priest and people pray privately. A song may be sung at this time.

Prayer After Communion

We stand. The priest invites us to pray with him as he asks God to help us live as God's People, the Body of Christ.

Priest: Let us pray…

People: Amen.

Concluding Rite

We stand for the concluding rite. The priest greets us, blesses us in the name of the Holy Trinity, and sends us forth to live as Jesus' disciples.

Greeting

Priest: The Lord be with you.

People: And also with you.

Blessing

Priest: May Almighty God bless you in the name of the Father, the Son, and the Holy Spirit.

People: Amen.

Dismissal

Priest: Go in peace to love and serve the Lord.

People: Thanks be to God.

We sing a hymn of praise. The priest kisses the altar as a sign of reverence. He and the other ministers leave in procession.

Holy Communion

Rules for Receiving Holy Communion

- Only baptized Catholics may receive Communion.

- To receive Holy Communion, we must be in the state of grace, free from mortal sin. If we have sinned mortally, we must first go to the Sacrament of Reconciliation and receive absolution before receiving Holy Communion. When we are sorry for our venial sins, receiving Holy Communion frees us from them.

- To honor the Lord, we fast for one hour before the time we receive Communion. This means we go without food or drink, except water or medicine.

- Catholics are required to receive Holy Communion at least once a year during Easter time. But we are encouraged to receive Communion every time we participate in the Mass.

How to Receive Communion

When we receive Jesus in Holy Communion, we welcome him by showing reverence. These steps can help you.

- Fold your hands, and join in the singing as you wait in line.

- When it is your turn, you can receive the Body of Christ in your hand or on your tongue.

- When you are shown the Eucharist, bow in reverence.

- To receive the Body of Christ in your hand, hold your hands out with the palms up. Place one hand underneath the other, and cup your hands slightly.

- To receive the Host on your tongue, fold your hands, open your mouth, and put your tongue out.

- The person who offers you Communion will say, "The Body of Christ." You say, "Amen." The priest, deacon, or extraordinary minister of Holy Communion places the Host in your hand or on your tongue. Step aside, and chew and swallow the host.

- You may choose to drink from the cup. When the cup is offered to you, the person will say, "The Blood of Christ." You say, "Amen." Take a small sip.

- Return to your place in church. Pray quietly in your own words. Thank Jesus for being with you.

Catholic Prayers

Lord's Prayer

Our Father, who art in heaven,
hallowed be thy name;
thy kingdom come;
thy will be done on earth as it is in heaven.
Give us this day our daily bread;
and forgive us our trespasses
as we forgive those who trespass against us;
and lead us not into temptation,
but deliver us from evil.
Amen.

Apostles' Creed

I believe in God, the Father almighty,
creator of heaven and earth.
I believe in Jesus Christ, his only Son, our Lord.
He was conceived by the power of
   the Holy Spirit
and born of the Virgin Mary.
He suffered under Pontius Pilate,
was crucified, died, and was buried.
He descended to the dead.
On the third day he rose again.
He ascended into heaven,
and is seated at the right hand of the Father.
He will come again to judge the living
   and the dead.
I believe in the Holy Spirit,
the holy catholic Church,
the communion of saints,
the forgiveness of sins,
the resurrection of the body,
and the life everlasting.
Amen.

Nicene Creed

We believe in one God, the Father,
  the Almighty,
  maker of heaven and earth,
  of all that is seen and unseen.
We believe in one Lord,
  Jesus Christ,
  the only Son of God,
  eternally begotten of the Father,
  God from God, Light from Light,
  true God from true God,
  begotten, not made, one in Being
    with the Father.
  Through him all things were made.
For us men and for our salvation
  he came down from heaven:
by the power of the Holy Spirit
  he was born of the Virgin Mary,
    and became man.
For our sake he was crucified under
  Pontius Pilate;
  he suffered, died, and was buried.
On the third day he rose
  again in fulfillment of
  the Scriptures;
he ascended into heaven and is
  seated at the right hand of
  the Father.
He will come again in glory
  to judge the living and the dead,
and his kingdom will have
  no end.
We believe in the Holy Spirit, the
  Lord, the giver of life,
  who proceeds from the Father
  and the Son.
With the Father and the Son he is
  worshiped and glorified.
He has spoken through the
  Prophets.
We believe in one holy
  catholic and apostolic Church.
We acknowledge one baptism for
  the forgiveness of sins.
We look for the resurrection of the
  dead, and the life of the world
  to come.
Amen.

Confiteor

I confess to Almighty God
and to you, my brothers and sisters,
that I have sinned through my own fault,
in my thoughts and in my words,
in what I have done,
and in what I have failed to do;
and I ask Blessed Mary ever virgin,
all the angels and saints,
and you, my brothers and sisters,
to pray for me to the Lord our God.

Gloria

Glory to God in the highest,
and peace to his people on earth.
Lord God, heavenly King,
almighty God and Father,
we worship you, we give you thanks,
we praise you for your glory.
Lord Jesus Christ, only Son of the Father,
Lord God, Lamb of God,
you take away the sin of the world:
have mercy on us;
you are seated at the right hand of the
Father:
receive our prayer.
For you alone are the Holy One,
you alone are the Lord,
you alone are the Most High,
Jesus Christ,
with the Holy Spirit,
in the glory of God the Father.
Amen.

Hail Mary

Hail, Mary, full of grace!
The Lord is with you!
Blessed are you among women,
and blessed is the fruit of your
   womb, Jesus.
Holy Mary, Mother of God,
pray for us sinners,
now and at the hour of our death.
Amen.

Come, Holy Spirit

Come, Holy Spirit, fill the hearts of your
   faithful
And kindle in them the fire of your love.
Send forth your Spirit and they shall be
   created.
And you shall renew the face of the earth.

Grace Before Meals

Bless us, O Lord, and these your gifts,
which we are about to receive
from your goodness.
Through Christ our Lord.
Amen.

Grace After Meals

We give you thanks for all your gifts,
almighty God,
living and reigning now and forever.
Amen.

Boldfaced numbers refer to pages on which the terms are defined.